GW00367684

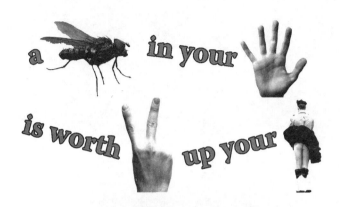

a [fly] in your [hand]

is worth [two] up your [kilt]

A MIDGE IN YOUR HAND IS WORTH TWO UP YOUR KILT

modern scottish proverbs

Stuart McLean

Crombie Jardine
Publishing Limited
4, Belgrave Place
Edinburgh
EH4 3AN
www.crombiejardine.com

This edition was first published by
Crombie Jardine Publishing Limited in 2007

ISBN 978-1-906051-06-8

Written by Stuart McLean

Typesetting and cover design
by Ben Ottridge

Printed and bound in China

Contents

Introduction

The Scottish language is rich in proverbs, sayings, maxims and wise aphorisms. Sadly, in the transition from the abacus to the computer, most of these have become outdated. This great little book thrusts these expressions into the 21st century providing millennia of wisdom in a practical modern format. It covers everything from bagpipes to whisky with a few mentions of our dear neighbours, the Sassenachs, thrown in.

So whether you are Scottish, a tourist visiting Scotland, an illegal immigrant gutting fish on Shetland or have found this book abandoned on a Trans-Siberian train, you are sure to be inspired and amused by our wit and wisdom.

The section on chat-up lines and insults will certainly help you, especially if you should you venture into a Scottish pub or nightclub, and could make the difference between getting a French kiss or a Glasgow kiss.

Website

For more information on Scottish proverbs please visit our website:

www.A-Midge-in-Your-Hand-is-Worth-Two-Up-Your-Kilt.com

Old Scottish
Proverbs Revamped

**When ye christen the bairn ye
should ken what to caa't.**

*Never arrange the christening until
the paternity suit is settled.*

Lang may yer lum reek.

*May your energy-efficient Baxi Boiler
continue to operate without the pilot
light extinguishing unexpectedly.*

**Better a sma' fish than
an empty dish.**
*It's better to eat well at McDonalds
than to wash dishes at the Ritz.*

**A bairn maun creep
afore it gangs.**
*A youngster must achieve its first
ASBO before it can be considered
worthy of membership to a gang.*

**The deil's aye guid tae
his ain kin.**
*Getting a bum deal from God? Tune
in and turn on to the Devil and you
could be this week's lottery winner.
(Note: All calls cost one soul – mobile
phone rates may vary.)*

What's for ye will no' go by ye.
*Anything that is for you will not go by
you – except the last bus home.*

A pennywecht o' love is worth a pund o' law.
An unhappy marriage is better than an expensive divorce.

As poor as a kirk mouse.
As poor as a Wester Hailes mouse the day after the dole money has been pissed against a wall.

Bairns speak i' the field what they hear i' the ha'.
Please Miss, ma maw's having an affair wi' the man next door . . . and so is ma da'.

Birds an' blethers fly.
*Carrier pigeons and emails
are great ways of spreading
malicious gossip.*

**The wan wi' the ladder's
as bad as the thief.**
*Never, ever trust your window
cleaner.*

**A guid word is as easy
sayed as an ill ane.**
*No, your bum does not
look big in that.*

**When poverty comes in
at the door love flies oot at
the windae.**
*It's easier to love an
arsehole of a lawyer than a
redundant plumber.*

**Try and mak friends
o' the unlikely.**
*Chat up a six-foot, gay, Chinese,
psychopathic lap-dancer today.*

Ane guid freend is worth mony relations.

A friend in need is a friend indeed. A relation in need is a distant relative.

Aye pat the richt end o' the wean.

It's hard to tell which end of an ugly child is which but as a rough guide the end that screeches is its head and the end that's covered in shit is its bum.

Even some Sassenachs are guid.

Some proverbs are complete bollocks.

Haud yer wheesht.
*Please press the pause button
on your larynx.*

**He's no' the happiest man that
has the maist gear.**
*It takes more than a 180-gear
bicycle to win the Tour de France.*

**Be ready wi' yer bunnet,
but slaw wi' yer purse.**
*Always leave the pub three minutes
before it's your round.*

A guid tale is no' the waur
o' bein' twice tauld.
*Damn! My senile dementia
is getting worse.*

He wad marry a midden
for the muck.
*If there were no eligible sheep
available, he would marry a dustbin
just to get the dowry of rancid waste.*

A fool may speer mair questions than a wise man can answer.
The SNP stagger the First Minister with the quantity if not the quality of their questions.

A fu' man an' a hungry horse aye mak haste hame.
A bevied man and an E-Type Jag always trigger the speed-cameras on the A77.

That'll no' set the heather licht.
Four gallons of kerosene and a box of Swan Vesta are no match for the Scottish rain.

Bonny birds is aye the warst singers.
Never marry a girl until you've heard her at a karaoke.

Ae man's meat is anither man's pushion.
Warning: May contain nuts.

Honest men dinnae carry salmon under their coats.
Men who tell the truth never catch fish and men who lie have very strange dress sense.

It's past joukin whan the heid's aff.
Queen Elizabeth turned to Mary and said "Just joking" only to discover that she was too late.

**Better sit idle than
wirk for nocht.**
*Even watching 'Trisha' repeats for ten
hours a day beats working in a burger
bar for a crap wage.*

**Dinnae streetch yer airm farther
than yer sleeve'll let ye.**
*The problem with expensive
designer clothes is that they never
bloody well fit.*

Dinnae trouble trouble till trouble troubles you.

Upon meeting an axe-carrying Ned in Sauchiehall Street avoid mentioning the fact that he's a useless prick.

Deid men dae nae herm.

Trust me, we'll come to no harm taking a midnight stroll through Greyfriars cemetery.

A man o' words, an' no' o' deeds, is like a garden fu' o' weeds.

Your MSP is as useful as a bag of rotting Ayrshires.

23

**A man o' mony trades may beg
his bread on Sunday.**
*A man may work all day as a dentist,
serve behind a bar in the evening
then drive a taxi all night but if his
wife watches QVC he'll still be skint at
the weekend.*

He winnae rive his faither's bunnet.

Generations of inbreeding has resulted in a medical condition whereby the people of Greenock have become incapable of wearing the traditional tartan bunnet worn by their forefathers. Instead they are forced to wear baseball caps at a jaunty angle.

A lucky man needs
little counsel.
The man who wins the lottery doesn't need Social Security handouts – but that certainly doesn't stop him claiming his weekly benefit payments.

A wolf may lose his teeth
but ne'er his nature.
A toothless Airdrieonian would suck you to death.

**Every man thinks his
ain craw blackest.**
*All right – so you think your
wife's an ugly bitch!*

**Dancin' like a hen on
a hot plate.**
*Taking part in 'Celebrity Come
Highland Dancing'.*

Dinnae lift me afore I fa'.
I'm not pissed – right!

**His mither cannae see
daylicht til him.**
*He's so bloody fat he fills the French
windows.*

**A midgie's as big as a
mountain, amaist.**
*The problem with bifocals is
that they make small things big and
big things small... but they're just
perfect for wearing during sex.*

28

**Better a fremmit freend nor
a freend fremmit.**
*It is better to find a stranger rather
than a best friend in bed with your
wife.*

**A man cannae bear a' his
ain kin about on his back.**
*Osteoarthritis is common in men
who persist in carrying their families
on their backs.*

I'll give you laldie!
I have an excess of laldie and would be delighted to make you the beneficiary of some of the superfluous accumulation.

A drink is shorter than a tale.
While reading the 'Complete Unabridged Poems and Songs of Robert Burns' one should be able to knock back at least six bottles of whisky and twenty-four cans of McEwan's ale.

**A fair maid tocherless will get
mair wooers than husbands.**
*Any lass that's not on Supplementary
Benefit will only attract scum.*

**Better be blythe wi' little
than sad wi' naething.**
*When you feel depressed at the size
of your manhood just think
of poor John Bobbitt.*

A fool can earn money, but it taks a wise man to keep it.
Computer programmers seldom marry.

Best to be off wi' the auld love before we be on wi' the new.
Take Liz Taylor's advice on how to have a long and happy marriage.

Choose yer wife on Setterday, no' on Sunday.
It's strange but true: women look much less hideous after ten pints of beer.

A guid day's darg may be done wi' a dirty spade.
It's possible to do a good day's hard labour even if there are crumbs on the computer keyboard.

A guid man maks a guid wife.
Now that gay marriages have become acceptable, your Mr Right could soon become your Mrs Right.

A gi'en game was ne'er won.
It was never a bloody penalty!

**A man may be kind, yet
gie little o' his gear.**
*Even a saint wouldn't part with his
Versace jeans.*

A horse hired never tired.
*It's okay to beat the crap out
of a hired car.*

As ae door's steekit anither opens.
Without double-glazing Highland cottages are so draughty it's impossible to keep all the doors closed against the gales.

Him that cheats me ance, shame faa him. Him that cheats me twice shame faa me.
If you ever speak to that bloody blonde barmaid again I'll cut your balls off.

**Ane would like to be lo'ed,
but wha would mool in wi' a
moudiewort?**
*Though it's good to be loved it is best
not to shack-up with a giant crab.*

Ane may think that daurna speak.
*Married men soon learn to keep their
mouths shut.*

Fair maidens wear nae purses.
*Face up to it guys: women never pay
for the drinks, the meal, the concert
ticket, the taxi, the condoms...*

**A hungersome wame
haes nae lugs.**
*Due to a bizarre genetic defect
amongst the people of Tiree
their ears spontaneously drop off
if they go without food for more
than a day.*

**A man may spit in his neive an'
do but little.**
*It takes more than a few gobs
of spittle for a footballer to
score a goal.*

God never measures men bi inches.
Even the most well-endowed men can be shit in bed.

A blind man needs nae looking-glass.
For goodness sake give some thought to what you buy people for Christmas.

Ma tongue isnae unner yer belt.
I don't do blow-jobs.

**Aw things haes an end, an'
a pudden haes twa.**
*Everything comes to an end, apart
from the wife's homemade black-
pudding which just seems to last an
eternity.*

**He left his silver in
his ither pootch.**
He's a mean old bastard.

As merry's a mautman.
*As merry as an Jedburgh Ned in a
field of marijuana.*

Gie yer tongue mair holidays than yer heid.
Shut up!

A bheil telebhisean agad?
We're from the Wee Free and are hunting down God-forsaking heathens.

Ilka body disnae hae the like o' that.
He seems to have contracted H5N1 Bird Flu.

**Better ne'er begun than
ne'er ended.**
*Never do anything today that you
can put off until tomorrow.*

**Better be freends a' a distance
than enemies a' hame.**
*The perfect divorce is one
that doesn't require a court
restraining order.*

Cast a cat ower the hoose an she'll fa' on her feet.
A cat thrown over a house will land on her feet – but her screeching is sure to attract the RSPCA.

Him that keeks thru' a keyhole micht see what will vex him.
Love does not stoop to spying – it hires a private detective.

Baked bread an' brown ale winnae bide lang.
Oh shit – I'm away to the lavie again!

Mony a mickle maks a muckle.
*Due to rampant inflation the muckle
has been revalued – there are now
385 mickles to the muckle.*

Rot him awa' wi' ham an' eggs.
*Don't risk murdering your man – give
him a coronary with greasy fry-ups
instead.*

**Beg frae beggars an'
you'll ne'er be rich.**
*Never ask a 'Big Issue' vendor
for your train fare home.*

43

Modern Scottish
Proverbs

A fool and his money are great companions on a night out.

An ASBO in time saves nine.

Familiarity breeds a lot of little bastards.

It's the early bird that gets first place in the dole queue.

If a job's worth doing, it's worth getting some other bugger to do it.

A friend in need is a bloody nuisance.

Wise men think what their wives tell them to think.

A red sky at night is a shepherd's delight. A red sky in the morning means you've had far too much Tequila Sunset.

God help the rich; the poor have the Department of Social Security.

46

Laugh and the world laughs with you, cry and you get thumped for being a wimp.

A dog is for life not just one sordid night of glorious sex.

If at first you don't succeed try, try and try to get someone else to do it.

'Scots, wha hae!' Aye we can sing a good song about freedom but let's draw the line at doing anything as drastic as breaking free from those 'chains and slaverie'.

Don't count your chickens in a Chinese restaurant.

Ne'er put up a Christmas light 'til August is out.

48

The early eagle catches
the early bird.

A sick-line a day keeps
the doctor away.

It's as difficult to get the
Poll Tax out of the Socialist as
it is to get the Socialist out
of the pub.

If you want to know if you'll still want sex in thirty years take a good hard look at your mother-in-law.

Never buy any pet that you couldn't take in a fight.

There's no fool like old Hamish McLachlan.

Sticks and stones may break my bones but age, sex and racial discrimination will be reported to the Equal Opportunities Commission.

Fighting for peace is like shagging for virginity.
(Banner at Faslane Peace Camp)

It is not advisable to place the sum total of your free-range poultry's production into the same wicker receptacle.

There are plenty more fish in the sea – unless you are impacted by regulation 'Sea Fishing (Restriction on Days at Sea) (No.2) (Amendment) Order 2004'.

A lie travels round the glens while truth is putting his trousers on.

Do not blame God for having created the Ned, but thank Him for not having given the little bugger your daughter's phone number.

A hand on a burd is worth
two on a bush.

If it wisnae for marriage, husband
and wives would hae to fight with
strangers.

Better late than pregnant.

The man who prizes his
penis disnae let his wife play
her bagpipes in bed.

A MIDGE IN YOUR HAND...

Oh you tak the high road and I'll
tak the low road and I'll hit the
M8 roadworks afore ye.

The computer is mightier
than the sword.

Don't look a gift beer
in the froth.

There's no advantage to be
derived from producing loud
screeches because of some fallen
white liquid that was extracted
from the lactic glands of a female
bovine.

Early to bed and early to
rise makes a man a bloody
pain in the arse to live with.

Finders keepers, losers insurance
claimants.

Flattery will get you
a good shag.

If it works use it. If it's
broke fix it. If it can't be
fixed sell it on eBay.

Never throw away a teabag 'til it's
seen twenty-two cups.

You cannot make a
silk sporran out of a
sow's testicles.

Man does not live by beer
alone – but it will get you through
two weeks on the Costa Brava.

A woman's wark will ne'er
be dune... for they tarry
tae lang at the boozers.

Marijuana makes the world
go round... and round...
and round...

People who live in glass houses
shouldn't use the lavie.

We'll never know the
worth of water till the
Irn Bru all runs dry.

Talk is cheap – except
with Vodafone.

You cannae shove yer grannie off
Ben Nevis without her gathering
moss.

Refrain from calculating the sum of your free-range, organic poultry prior to their incubation and emergence from their embryonic habitat.

Scottish Education is the best in the world – in fact 78% of those on the dole have got a first-class honours degree.

Honesty is the best policy – but
only as a last resort.

Haemoglobin is more
viscous than H2O.

Bagpipes

Bagpipes – an octopus
wearing a kilt.

The bagpipes are the best way to
terrorise the neighbours without
the inconvenience of getting an
ASBO.

To play the blues choose a
harmonica, to play despair choose
the bagpipes.

The difference between a piper
and a terrorist is that terrorists
have sympathisers.

Bagpipes and the Loch
Ness Monster have two things in
common – they attract tourists
and terrify little children.

A compassionate Scotsman
is one who can play the bagpipes
but doesn't.

There's nae difference between a bagpipe and an onion, except that nobody cries when they chop up a bagpipe.

The bagpipes and a squealing pig have much in common – the difference is that the pig has a purpose.

Give the piper a penny to play and two pence to bugger off.

Twelve supporters and one set of bagpipes make a Tartan Army.

If you want a woman who can give a great blow-job choose one who plays the bagpipes.

If the bagpipe doesn't kill you with its tentacles it will kill you with its screech.

The Haggis

Haggis – that icon of the Scottish nation; lungs, heart and liver of sheep with a dash of blood stuffed into a sheep's stomach! No wonder we're always so bloody miserable.

A haggis a day keeps those damn vegetarians away.

Haggis is akin to road kill but without the legs.

A MIDGE IN YOUR HAND...

You can take a haggis to water but you cannae drown the wee bugger.

If the haggis sees his shadow we will have six more weeks of winter.

If he doesn't see his shadow we will have an early spring.
(Folklore for predicting the weather that is used on the 25th of January, Haggis Day)

When haggis is in season it can
easily be shot but out of season
the game-keepers do plot.
*(Traditional saying amongst haggis
hunters.)*

Haggii in the heather
fuck together.

You cannot prevent the haggii of
sorrow from running up your legs,
but you can prevent them from
building nests in your underwear.

The Kilt

The kilt is the national dress of the Scottish wedding.

Beware Englishmen in kilts and beggars wearing gold.

There are two occasions when a kilt just can't be beaten: when you're up close with a girl and when you've got a dose of diarrhoea.

Men in kilts shouldnae practise the Highland fling in fields o' thistles.

Taking Viagra while wearing
the kilt is a sure-fire way of
getting arrested for indecent
behaviour.

It's an ill wind that blows
up yer kilt.

A washed kilt is like a broken leg,
you can't do a fling with it.

It's easier to let your
'wind blow free' when you're
wearing a kilt.

Let the wind blow high,
let the wind blow low, through
the streets in my kilt I'll streak.

There's nought worn under a
Scotsman's kilt; everything is in
perfect working order.

The Loch Ness Monster

There's not a haggis within six miles of Loch Ness – sure proof that there's a haggis-eating monster living in the loch.

There will be a monster in Loch Ness for as long as there are gullible American tourists.

Sightings of the Loch Ness Monster rise in direct proportion to local whisky consumption.

If you have the choice between being attacked by Nessie or being attacked by midges, choose Nessie every time.

Ah believe in the Loch Ness Monster. Ah believe in flying saucers. Ah believe in flower fairies. Ah believe that, one day, the people of Scotland will have the guts to rise up and be a nation again.

Nessie keeps well hidden for she knows the reputation of the local sheep farmers.

The Midge

A midge in your hand is
worth two up your kilt.

The midge's bite is
worse than its bark.

Scaled up, the midge is more
lethal than a nuclear warhead.

Unscrupulous creature the midge
– it will happily bite the hand that
feeds it.

For every tourist the Scottish
Tourist Board attracts the mighty
midge chases three away.

Whisky and
Drinking

Alcohol may be the road
to nowhere, but at least it's
the scenic route.

Warning: whisky can seriously
damage your wallet.

Whisky: making women look
sexier since 1492.

There's no harm in the occasional
binge sobriety provided you don't
make a habit of it.

Whisky will cure any ailment, and what it won't cure isn't worth catching.

Don't drown your sorrows in your whisky, it spoils the flavour.

Highland women are not the prettiest in the world, in fact if it weren't for whisky there would be negative population growth.

Two wrongs don't make a right but two whiskies will help you enjoy your wrongs.

Never drink whisky without water or water without whisky.

With every glass that's downed friends become friendlier and enemies become friendlier too.

Oh! Campbeltown Loch, Ah wish ye were 30-year-old Balvenie Single Barrel Malt!

Whisky – cheaper
than therapy.

A day without whisky is like a
lifetime without hippopotami.

Avoid a hangover – take the 'hair
of the dog' and repeat at
15 minute intervals.

Buckfast – yer other
nashunal drink.

Whisky is not the answer
to your problems – whisky is the
question.

He could drink for his country – if
only it were an Olympic sport.

Rangers supporters drink to
drown their sorrows. Celtic
supporters drink to celebrate
their successes. Partick Thistle
supporters drink in an effort to
remember when they last scored
a goal.

A MIDGE IN YOUR HAND...

If you think a whisky glass is half full you are an optimist, if you think it half empty you are an alcoholic.

Don't use whisky to drown your sorrows – stick her in a bath of freezing water.

Employment and
Unemployment

It's tough work staying idle.

They can take away our shipbuilding, they can take away our coal mining, they can take away our car industry but they can never, ever take away our right to receive our dole giro.

Work is what fills those awful gaps between flunking school and winning the lottery.

If you don't sow in the spring you won't have the hassle of reaping in the autumn.

Sign on, drink away your dole money, moan about immigrants taking all our jobs.

Only fools and horses work; the rest make do with Family Support, Unemployment Benefit, Disability Benefits, Multiple Addiction Supplementary Benefit, Bereavement Benefits, Cold Weather Payments, Crisis Loans, Incapacity Benefit, Industrial Injuries Disablement Benefit, Jobseeker's Allowance, Maternity Allowance and numerous other payments.

Make hay while the sun shines
then do bugger all for the other
fifty-one weeks.

Scottish Weather

Land of the hill and heather,
Land of the awful weather,
Land where the midges gather
– Scotland the grave.

If you don't like the weather close
the front door.

The only time it's not raining in
Glencoe is when it's snowing.

When the eagle soars high, foul
weather; when the eagle soars
low, foul weather.

A MIDGE IN YOUR HAND...

When the rain turns from
torrential to bucketing then there
be summer.

There are three signs of summer:
mad Americans wandering
through your garden; corncrake
rasping through the night; and
warm, torrential rain.
(Iona adage)

Save your money for a rainy day
and you'll die poor.

Scottish Frugality

Charity begins at home – your neighbour's home.

The only extravagance he has is his excessive meanness.

He's as generous as a starving dog with half a bone.

The end justifies the meanness.

Two can live as cheaply as one – if they move in with the parents.

Avoid spending money – staple it
into your sporran.

She wouldnae gie a smile to a
baby panda doing a jig for charity
on a hot air balloon.

Oh Lord, I do not ask that you
give me wealth, just show me
where it's hidden.

What use is love? It can't
buy you money.

A MIDGE IN YOUR HAND...

A penny spent is a fortune lost.

There's plenty of point in crying over spilt whisky.

Where there's a will there's a way to hoodwink some of the inheritance.

England and
the English

Englishman: someone who thinks haggis is weird but Morris dancing normal.

God gave the Scots whisky, spectacular mountains and beautiful glens as compensation for having the English as neighbours.

An Englishman's home is his Scottish castle.

Take away our mountains, our lochs and our glens and what have you got? England.

Better the devil you know than the Sassenach you don't know.

Glasgow
v
Edinburgh

An Edinburgher who's handy with a blade is called a butcher – a Weegie who's handy with a blade is called a thug.

An Edinburgher who likes flowers is called a horticulturalist – a Weegie who likes flowers is called a poof.

A Weegie who's handy with a spade is called a gardener – an Edinburgher who's handy with a spade is called a grave robber.

A MIDGE IN YOUR HAND...

In for a penny, in for a pound.
*(Comparison of the cost of using the
toilets in slummy Glasgow with that of
posh Edinburgh.)*

Glasgow is the friendly city – a
Ned there will give you a smile
as he relieves you of your wallet.
Edinburgh Neds just nick your
wallet without even a polite word
of abuse.

Edinburgh has the Royal Mile,
Glasgow has the loyal smile.

Scottish
Chat-Up Lines

Unisex Chat-Ups

Can Ah buy ye a drink, or would ye rather have the money?

If you wis a bogie Ah would pick you first.

Ah'm really, really pissed, gonnae take me hame?

If Ah said you had a body like a Scottish-Blackface would you hold it against me?

106

Fancy going halves on a bastard?

Càite bheil an taigh beag?

Do you take Visa?

Are ye going to finish that drink
or can Ah have it?

Would ye like tae come
back tae ma place tae see
ma retchings?

A MIDGE IN YOUR HAND...

Didn't we go tae different schools
ragether?

You look awfully familiar –
are you a porn star?

You're as ugly as shit
but Ah'm desperate.

Does this smell like chloroform
to you?

Let's go hunt for
some wild asparagus.

Hi, your mum just phoned, Ah've
to take you home.

Are you free tonight or do
Ah have to pay?

Are ye a Tim or a Hun?

Chat-Ups For Men

If ye wannae learn to play
the bagpipes ye can practise
oan ma cock.

Dae ye believe in sex
at first sight?

You look exactly like
ma ex-wife.

Hi, ma mates call me 'Nessie' cos
Ah'm huge and enigmatic.

Nice legs, hen – what time
dae they open?

Fancy a shag, sweetheart – or
could ye just lie down while Ah
have one?

How do ye like yer eggs
in the morning, scrambled
or fertilized?

Whit's a slut like you dayin'
in a classy joint like this?

Dae ye fancy a vodka
and ketamine?

Now thit Ah've goat a couple o'
Scotch in me, how wid you like
some Scotch in you?

Ah'm a virgin – well if ye
don't count a couple of
sheep and a parrot.

See you doll, you don't
sweat much fur a fat bird!

Gonnae toss ma
cabber fur me?

Ma doctor said thit
Ah'm gonnae die if Ah
don't get a shag today.

Baa... baa... what's a
nice sheep like you doing
in a field like this?

Wid ye like tae do a highland fling
on my cabber?

A MIDGE IN YOUR HAND...

Hi, ma mates call me 'Big Mac'
cos Ah've got a quarter pounder.

See me hen, Ah'm on the dole,
Ah'm an alcoholic and a drug
addict but maybe Ah could be
your mister perfect.

Chat-Ups For Women

Ah love you so Ah do,
gonnae marry me and gie
me loads o' weans?

Have ye got a cabber
under yer kilt or are ye jist
a randy bugger?

Ma mates dared me tae
chat you up so they did.

That's a massive sporran you've
goat – is it loaded?

Gonnae take yer tongue outae
ma mouth?

Ah'm allergic tae nutmeg.

Kin Ah see yer wee, sleekit,
cowrin, tim'rous beastie?

We are whit we eat...
Ah'm fast, cheap and easy.

Donald where's yer trousers…
are ye no' frozen staunin' there in
ra scud?

Gonnae buy me drinks 'til
you stop looking ugly.

Ah've lost ma virginity – huv ye
seen it anywhere?

Ah'm new in town. Could
ye give me directions to
ra VD Clinic?

A MIDGE IN YOUR HAND...

Take me… ay gonnae?

Show me yer hairy haggis and
Ah'll show ye ma badger.

Who wis that sheep Ah saw ye
with last night?

Hey ya big bastard stop looking at
ma tits.

Shite – Ah'm gonnae be sick.

Scottish Insults

A MIDGE IN YOUR HAND...

Ye've goat a face like a
hen shitting razors.

He's two kilts short of a
Highland wedding.

He's goat a face like a dug trying
tae shag a thistle.

She's pumping the treadle but her
spinning wheel isnae turning.

He's one kilt pin short
of a full streak.

His head's on top o' Ben Nevis
but his arse is in the Glen.

Help ma boab she's as sexy as a
lamb after ten pints o' Tennents.

She's as enticing as Campbeltown
Loch without the whisky.

She comes from Maryhill – where
virgins are an endangered
species.

His parentage is as dubious
as the Stone of Destiny.

His quaich disnae fill o' the
way tae the brim.

Yer so stupid ya big bauchle ye
couldnae even button up yer kilt.

His head's fu' o' half-fermented
barley.

Her face has as much paint
as the Forth Road Bridge.

He's two Gay Gordons
short of a ceilidh.

She's as dynamic as a
grub in mashed neeps.

He's three tassels short
of a sporran.

She was dragged up the
Clyde in the jobbie dredger.

He's got all the luck o' white
heather in a heath fire.

She's got a bum that's
bigger than the QE2.

Her farting sounds like a
dirge on the bagpipes.

The stove is on, but her tatties
arnae cooking.

He's twelve crates of
beer short of a party.

He's not so much the 'Great
chieftain o' the puddin-race' as
'Greetin' big-wean wi'
the puddin-face'.

He looks like a half shut knife at a
gang-fight on Glasgow Green.

She's two running rhinos short of
a full marathon.

He's as cheery as a social worker
on dole day.

A MIDGE IN YOUR HAND...

She's six Irn-Bru short
of the dozen.

He's two white stripes
short of a saltire.

She's as graceful as a
hippopotamus doing the
highland fling.

The wheel's spinning, but
his haggis is dead.

She's a few threads short
of a tartan rug.

Jings she came face to face
wi' the Loch Ness Monster and it
goat a terrible fright.

He has an intellect rivalled only by
a plate o' tatties.

She's got all the charisma of a
single-barrel malt that's been
mixed wi' cherry cola.

He's two haggii short of
a Burns Supper.

Yer makin' as much
sense as a half-pun o'
mince on a motorbike.

He's no' the sharpest
Skein Dubh in the hose.

Aberdonian
Proverbs

It is better to have loved a sheep
and lost than never to have loved
a sheep at all.

Don't bite the hand that
feeds you.
(Warning sign in DHSS office.)

He's so quick he can ejaculate in
two shakes of a pig's tail.

130

Give a man from Peterhead a fish, and he'll eat for a day. Teach him how to fish and he'll forever moan about cod quotas.

May as well be hanged for a sheep as a lamb – damn these bestiality laws.

There's o'er muckle guid loons an quines in yon chiel's class, but jist a puckle gifted anes.

Talk of the devil and a Buckie bumpkin is sure to appear.

Nooadays loons an quines dinna daunce wi een anither, they daunce at een anither.

Do you think I came Doon the Dee on a digestive?
(I may look dumb but I can count up to ten pigs without using my fingers.)

You can take the sheep out of Aberdeen, but you will never take the Aberdonian out of the sheep.

A left-handed Aberdonian keeps all his money in his right pocket.

I, Angus, take ewe, Dolly-the-Sheep, as my lawful wedded wife.

Dundonian
Proverbs

Ehm no'n eejit, shirsels'n eejit.
(I'm not an idiot, it's yourself who's the idiot.)

It takes a thief to catch a thief.
(Dundee Police recruitment campaign.)

Laughter is the best medicine.
(Sign outside recently closed hospital.)

A MIDGE IN YOUR HAND...

Cahlm doon, yeh big
fairdeegowk yeh!
(Chill man – have some hash.)

Never ask a left-handed
Dundonian to open a right-
handed tin.

Too many Arbrothians
spoil the Arbroath.

Love your neighbour – just don't
let the wife know.
*(Popular saying in the
Tayside area.)*

A Dundonian who has lost
the will to live is called a Dundee
United fan.

Edinburghian
Proverbs

Wise men come from the East
and all the cowboys from the
West.

Beware of Glaswegians
bearing gifts.

Better marry ower the midden
than ower the muir.
*(It's better to marry a girl from the
slums of Craigmillar than a rich bitch
from Berwick.)*

You can take the piss out of the Glaswegians but you can't take the Glaswegians out of the piss.

A dog is not just for Christmas – there should be enough left over for sandwiches on Boxing Day.
(Wester Hailes saying)

The Scottish Parliament wisnae built in a day and wi' bugger all change ootae £431 million.

A Glaswegian is a man
who keeps the Sabbath, and
everything else he can
lay his hands on.

A Wee-Weegie is a drunk who
hasn't yet celebrated
his twelfth birthday.

The only good thing that comes
out of Glasgow is the 5:22 train
back to Edinburgh.

Some Weegies are born mediocre, some Weegies achieve meritocracy but most Weegies stagger there through years of dedicated drinking.

Glaswegian
Proverbs

Do ye think I came up ra Clyde
oan a banana boat?
*(I may look stupid but I have a 3rd
Class Honours degree in Business
Administration from Caledonian
University.)*

I belang tae Glasgow, dear
old Glasgow toon.

But there's something the matter
wi' Glasgow, for a flat cost a
hundred-thousand poons.

No man ever steps in the River
Clyde twice.
*(Those that live in the penthouse
apartments along the river can testify
that the mildly diluted toxic waste
that masquerades as a river will kill
anyone who gets within breathing
distance.)*

There's nowt so queer as Partick
Thistle fans.

It's better to give than to receive.
(Sign outside Glasgow VD Clinic.)

A closed mouth catches
no flies – so open wide
and enjoy your supper.
(Easterhouse saying)

Who lies with Airdrieonians shall
rise up with fleas.
(Clydebank Football Club slogan.)

Every cloud has a gold lining.
*(Popular saying in the affluent suburb
of Milngavie.)*

After clouds comes fair weather.
*(It pisses down all year – but see
the Glasgow Fair it's always smashin'
doon at Largs.)*

**Glasgow smiles better – after a
few buckets o' beer.**

**Wan fur the road an put
it oan ra slate ma man.**
*(I shall take another double whisky
but as I seem to have forgotten
my Platinum American Express
card could I delay reimbursement
until I find myself some gainful
employment?)*

Highland and
Island Proverbs

Blood is thicker than
water but it fair mucks
up your whisky.

One good turn
deserves a ceilidh.

Abair sin, nuair a chaitheas
tu cruach mhòine còmhla ris.
*(Where the hell did I put
my false teeth?)*

Love me, love my sheep.

149

A MIDGE IN YOUR HAND...

It's easier to woo a coo
than a woman; they need much
less ketamine.

If you can't see Ben Nevis it's
raining – if you can see Ben Nevis
it's about to rain.
(Fort William saying)

Inverness – where men are men
and sheep are nervous.

The rain in Skye falls
mainly on the head.

A red sky at night is a shepherd's delight. A red sky in the morning – Dounreay issues a warning.

It's a wise mouse that nestles in a Shetland man's wallet.

There are two seasons on Orkney – June and winter.

Ner cast a clout 'til ye get tae ra lap dance club.
(Following complaints from British Rail, this expression became popular amongst strippers in Ullapool that they should refrain from practising their routines on busy commuter trains.)

Put a Lowlander in a kilt and he'll automatically gravitate towards the nearest wedding reception.

152

A rich man has mair cousins than
his faither had kin.
*(Inbreeding in Elgin has reached
abominable proportions.)*

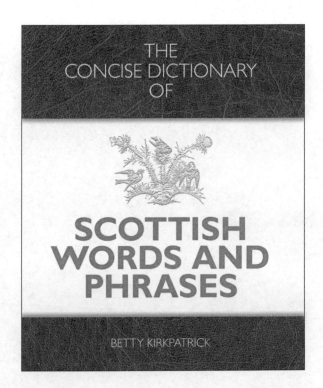

THE
CONCISE DICTIONARY
OF

SCOTTISH
WORDS AND
PHRASES

BETTY KIRKPATRICK

ISBN 978-1-905102-88-4, £4.99, pb

THE
CONCISE DICTIONARY
OF

SCOTTISH
QUOTATIONS

BETTY KIRKPATRICK

ISBN 978-1-905102-89-1, £4.99, pb

Other Scottish interest titles

Auld Scottish Grannies' Remedies
ISBN-10: 1-905102-06-2
ISBN-13: 978-1-905102-06-8
£2.99, pb

The Book of Scottish Patriotism
ISBN-10: 1-905102-29-1
ISBN-13: 978-1-905102-29-7
£4.99, pb

The Concise Dictionary of
Scottish Words and Phrases
ISBN-10: 1-905102-88-7
ISBN-13: 978-1-905102-88-4
£4.99, pb

The Concise Dictionary of
Scottish Quotations
ISBN-10: 1-905102-89-5
ISBN-13: 978-1-905102-89-1
£4.99, pb

The Concise Dictionary of Great Scots
ISBN-10: 1-905102-31-3
ISBN-13: 978-1-905102-31-0
£4.99, hb

Greyfriars Bobby
ISBN-10: 1-905102-04-6
ISBN-13: 978-1-905102-04-4
£2.99, pb

Haggis, Hogmanay and Halloween
ISBN-10: 1-905102-32-1
ISBN-13: 978-1-905102-32-7
£2.99, pb

Jockney Rhyming Slang
ISBN-10: 1-905102-85-2
ISBN-13: 978-1-905102-85-3
£2.99, pb

The Little Book of Neds
ISBN-10: 1-905102-30-5
ISBN-13: 978-1-905102-30-3
£2.99, pb

Ned Jokes
ISBN-13: 978-1-906051-05-1
£2.99, pb

Ned Speak
ISBN-10: 1-905102-73-9
ISBN-13: 978-1-905102-73-0
£2.99, pb

Nessie
ISBN-10: 1-905102-05-4
ISBN-13: 978-1-905102-05-1
£2.99, pb

Scottish Wit & Wisdom
ISBN-13: 978-1-906051-13-6
£5.99, hb

www.crombiejardine.com